THE SCIENCE OF
WATER

PROJECTS AND EXPERIMENTS WITH WATER SCIENCE & POWER

Bibliographical Note

TABLETOP SCIENTIST: THE SCIENCE OF WATER, Projects and Experiments with Water Science and Power, first published by Dover Publications, Inc., in 2013, is an unabridged reprint of the work originally produced by David West Children's Books, London, in 2005. The text has been revised to conform to American spelling and vocabulary.

International Standard Book Number

ISBN-13: 978-0-486-49262-9
ISBN-10: 0-486-49262-1

Manufactured in China
49262101
www.doverpublications.com

TABLETOP SCIENTIST: THE SCIENCE OF WATER
was produced by

David West 🏃 Children's Books
7 Princeton Court
55 Felsham Road
London SW15 1AZ

Designer: Rob Shone
Editor: Gail Bushnell
Picture Research: Gail Bushnell

PHOTO CREDITS :
Abbreviations: t-top, m-middle, b-bottom, r-right,
l-left, c-centre.

Pages 14-15 (M Watson) – Ardea London Ltd. 4t, 6r,18l, 20t, 22tl, 28tl – Corbis Images. $m, 6l, 8 both, 12l, 20m, 22–23 – Digital Stock. 16 (Dietmar Nill) – naturepl.com. 12m (Pacific Press Services); 26t (Julianm Makey) – Rex Features Ltd.

Every effort has been made to contact copyright holders of any material reproduced in this book. Any omissions will be rectified in subsequent printings if notice is given to the publishers.

With special thanks to the models: Meshach Burton, Sam Heming De-Allie, Annabel Garnham, Andrew Gregson, Hannah Holmes, Molly Rose Ibbett, Margaux Monfared, Max Monfared, Charlotte Moore, Beth Shon, Meg Shon, William Slater, Danielle Smale and Pippa Stannard.

An explanation of difficult words can be found in the glossary on page 31.

TABLETOP SCIENTIST

THE SCIENCE OF
WATER

PROJECTS AND EXPERIMENTS
WITH WATER SCIENCE & POWER

STEVE PARKER

DOVER PUBLICATIONS, INC.
Mineola, New York

CONTENTS

From water as a gas...

...to water as a solid...

...to water as we usually see it, a liquid – this substance affects our lives in countless ways. Are you feeling thirsty yet?

INTRODUCTION

Water is everywhere—gushing from the tap, floating high above as drops in clouds, falling as rain, lying around in puddles and ponds, and rushing along rivers to the ocean. We also see water in nonliquid form, as solid ice in ice cubes and on ponds. Water can be a gas or vapor. It is all around us in the air. Too much makes the weather feel humid or "sticky." Water is useful for washing, cleaning, and cooking. Most important, water is vital for all life. The human body is two-thirds water. We need a supply of clean, fresh water every day. All of these topics and processes, and many more, rely on our knowledge of the science of water.

HOW IT WORKS

These panels explain the scientific ideas in each project and the processes that make it work.

Where you see these symbols:

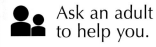

Ask an adult to help you.

Sharp tools may be needed.

Project to be done outdoors.

Prepare work surface for a messy project.

Prepare each project carefully and follow the instructions. Remember: real scientists always put safety first.

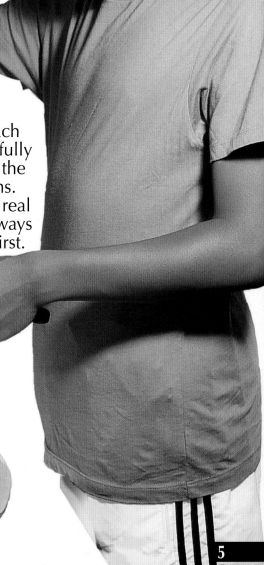

TRY IT AND SEE

These panels give you more ideas to try, so you can experiment and find out more about water.

The water cycle is driven by two main forces. The sun's heat causes water vapor to rise high into the air. Gravity pulls it back down as rain and makes rivers flow and waterfalls cascade down cliffs.

WATER CYCLE

Water is so common, yet the amount of "new" water made every day is tiny. So is the amount of water destroyed. Most of the time, it's the same water moving along, going around and around. This is known as the water cycle. The water that came out of your tap today might fall on your head next week as rain!

Clouds are billions of tiny water droplets light enough to float. They clump together as larger drops and fall as rain.

PROJECT: MAKE A RAIN CLOUD

RAIN CLOUD

WHAT YOU NEED

- plastic drink bottle
- stiff wire
- cardboard
- cardboard box
- ice cubes
- tape
- scissors
- beaker

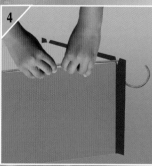
1 CAREFULLY CUT THE TOP END FROM A PLASTIC DRINK BOTTLE.

2 TAKE TWO LENGTHS OF STIFF WIRE, BEND EACH END INTO A U-SHAPE TO HOLD THE BOTTLE.

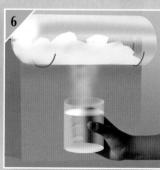
3 CUT SOME CARDBOARD TO MAKE THE "SKY" BACKGROUND. CUT TWO NOTCHES FOR THE WIRES.

4 FIX THE CARDBOARD TO A LARGE BOX. TAPE THE WIRE "CRADLES" IN PLACE.

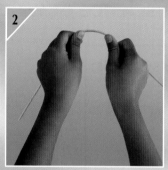
5 FILL THE BOTTLE WITH ICE CUBES OR CRUSHED ICE. PUT IT IN THE "CRADLES."

6 FILL A BEAKER WITH WARM TAP WATER, PLACE UNDER THE BOTTLE, AND WATCH.

THE WARM WATER GIVES OFF
INVISIBLE GAS, WATER VAPOR.
BECAUSE THIS IS HOT IT RISES.
WHEN IT TOUCHES THE COLD
BOTTLE IT CONDENSES, OR
TURNS BACK TO LIQUID
WATER, AND DRIPS BACK
DOWN AS "RAINDROPS."

THE WATER CYCLE

Water constantly moves or
circulates between oceans, air,
and land. It changes from liquid water
to vapor when heated by the sun, and
back again as it rises into cold air.
This liquid water returns to the
surface as rain and snow, flows
back down to the ocean,
and the cycle continues.

WATER CONDENSES AND
FALLS AS RAIN OR FREEZES
INTO SNOW

WATER SEEPS
INTO THE GROUND
AND FLOWS SLOWLY

WATER VAPOR IS GIVEN
OFF BY VEGETATION AND
EVAPORATES FROM LAKES

WATER VAPOR IS BLOWN INLAND

WATER FLOWS ALONG STREAMS AND
RIVERS AND RETURNS TO THE OCEAN

HEAT FROM THE SUN EVAPORATES WATER

SOLID WATER

Icebergs float low in the water with only about the top one-eighth showing.

Water is heavy, but not all water weighs the same. The same bucket full of cold water weighs slightly more than one full of hot water. This is because water shrinks or contracts as it cools, so there's more in a full bucket when it's cold. But this happens only down to 40 °F. At 32 °F, water becomes solid and gets bigger again!

Below 32 °F, water turns from its liquid form into a hard, glassy solid. We say that the water freezes into ice.

PROJECT: MELT A MINI-ICEBERG

MINI-ICEBERG

WHAT YOU NEED

- drink bottle
- ice cube tray
- two different colors of food colouring
- scissors

MIX A FEW DROPS OF FOOD COLORING INTO SOME WATER IN AN ICE CUBE TRAY. FREEZE THIS OVERNIGHT TO MAKE YOUR MINI-ICEBERG.

CUT THE TOP OFF OF A BOTTLE. MIX SOME FOOD COLORING INTO SOME WATER AND ALMOST FILL THE BOTTLE. DROP IN THE MINI-ICEBERG.

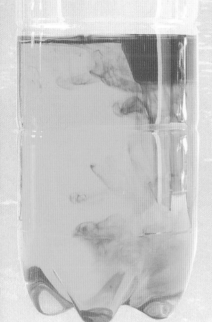

DOWN AND UP

The warmer water around the cube melts the ice. At first this melted-ice water is colder and heavier, or denser, than the water around it, so it sinks down through the surrounding water. Gradually it mixes with the surrounding water, warms, and begins to rise. This is why the food coloring from the melted ice sinks and then rises.

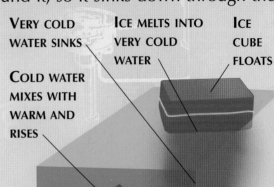

VERY COLD WATER SINKS

COLD WATER MIXES WITH WARM AND RISES

ICE MELTS INTO VERY COLD WATER

ICE CUBE FLOATS

FLOATING, SINKING, FLOATING AGAIN?

WATER CONTINUES TO EXPAND OR GET BIGGER AS IT FREEZES INTO ICE. SO ICE IS LIGHTER, OR LESS DENSE, THAN THE SAME VOLUME OF WATER (SEE NEXT PAGE). THIS IS WHY ICE CUBES AND ICEBERGS FLOAT. SOON THE WATER'S WARMTH AROUND THE CUBE TURNS THE ICE BACK INTO WATER. WE SAY THAT THE ICE MELTS. WATCH THE COLORED WATER FROM THE MELTING ICE. WHERE DOES IT GO AND WHY?

BURST A BOTTLE?

The power of water as it expands when freezing into ice is amazing. Fill a plastic drink bottle with water and place it in the freezer overnight. Next day, see how the expanding ice has split the bottle!

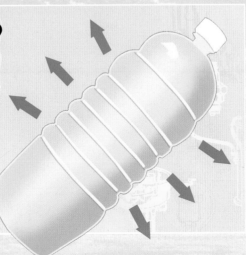

HEAVY AND THICK

An important feature of water is that, like all liquids, it has density, which is the amount of water in a certain volume. In fact water is so common that the scientific density scale is based on it. Its density is 1.

A hydrometer is useful in helping to keep a healthy environment in a salt water aquarium. By measuring its density you can gauge just how salty the water is.

PROJECT: A SIMPLE HYDROMETER (DENSITY MEASURER)

HYDROMETER

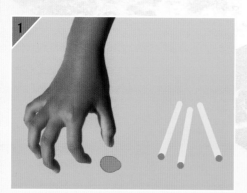

CUT THREE EQUAL LENGTHS OF DRINKING STRAW 2 INCHES LONG. TAKE A SMALL BALL OF MODELING CLAY.

ATTACH THE CLAY TO THE END OF ONE STRAW. PLACE IT IN A JAR OF WATER TO SEE HOW DEEP IT FLOATS.

WHAT YOU NEED

- modeling clay
- drinking straws
- jelly jars
- liquids to test
- scissors

ADJUST THE AMOUNT OF CLAY SO ABOUT ONE-THIRD OF THE STRAW FLOATS ABOVE THE SURFACE.

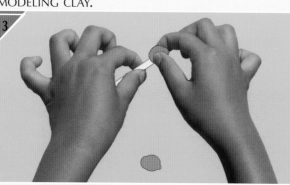

MAKE TWO MORE CLAY BALLS THE SAME SIZE AND WEIGHT. ATTACH THEM TO THE OTHER STRAWS. PREPARE TEST LIQUIDS SUCH AS WATER, HONEY, AND COOKING OIL.

WHICH IS DENSER?
PUT THE HYDROMETERS
IN THE TEST LIQUIDS.
THE DENSER THE
LIQUID, THE
MORE IT PRESSES
UP ON THE STRAW
AND CLAY, SO THE
HIGHER THEY FLOAT.
LESS DENSE LIQUIDS
LET THE HYDROMETER
SINK LOWER.

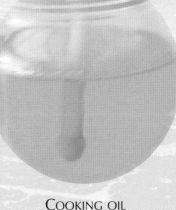

HONEY · COOKING OIL · COLORED WATER

PARTICLES PACKED IN

Density is the mass of a substance in a certain volume. We usually measure mass as weight. Cooking oil is less dense than water. But does it flow faster or slower than water? And which substance tends to stick to the sides of the jar more?

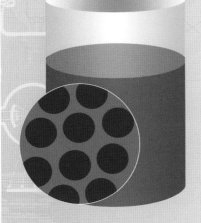

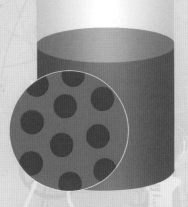

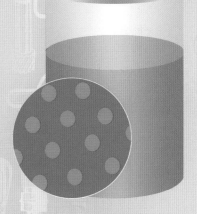

HONEY (MOST DENSE) · **WATER (MEDIUM DENSITY)** · **COOKING OIL (LEAST DENSE)**

LIQUID LAYERS

Try slowly pouring some honey into one of the empty jars to make a 3/4-inch layer on the bottom. Add a 3/4-inch layer of water dyed with a food coloring. Pour it in gently over the back of a spoon held just above the honey, so it hardly splashes. Finally do the same with a 3/4-inch layer of cooking oil. Do the three colored layers stay separate because of their different densities?

WHAT HAPPENS IF YOU POUR THE LIQUIDS INTO THE JAR IN A DIFFERENT ORDER?

DISAPPEARING INTO WATER

By looking at water, you cannot tell if it is pure or if it has substances like salt or sugar in it. Such substances dissolve, which means they split up into their tiniest particles, molecules, that are too small to see. These molecules float about among water's own molecules.

Sea water's taste shows that salt is dissolved in it. This makes it more dense, so it's easier to float in than water in a swimming pool.

As shallow salty water dries in the hot sun, it leaves its salt behind. People dig it up and use it in industry and for cooking as sea salt or rock salt.

PROJECT: THE MID-WATER FISH FLOATER

FISH FLOATER

WHAT YOU NEED

- potato slice
- plastic sheet
- drink bottle
- salt
- food coloring
- scissors

1. CAREFULLY CUT A TRIANGLE TAIL AND MOON-SHAPED FIN FROM A PLASTIC SHEET.

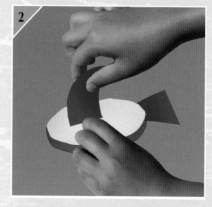

2. MAKE A SLIT THROUGH THE POTATO SLICE AND ONE AT THE EDGE. SLOT FINS INTO PLACE.

3. ADD SALT TO TAP WATER IN A JAR AND STIR. REPEAT UNTIL NO MORE SALT CAN DISSOLVE.

TWO LAYERS

Salt water has salt molecules in it as well as water molecules. This makes it more dense than the pure fresh tap water, so it forms a layer underneath. The fish is heavy enough to sink in fresh water, but the denser salt water holds it up.

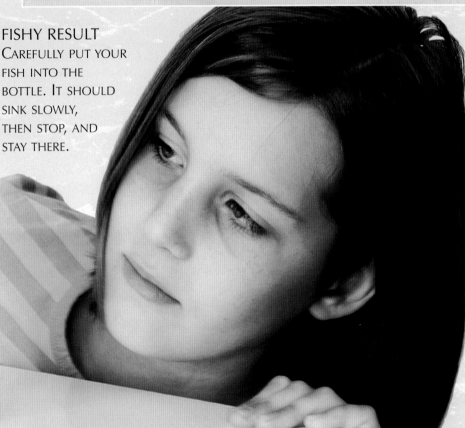

FRESH WATER

SALT WATER

FISHY RESULT
CAREFULLY PUT YOUR FISH INTO THE BOTTLE. IT SHOULD SINK SLOWLY, THEN STOP, AND STAY THERE.

HALF FILL THE BOTTLE WITH THE SALT WATER. POUR TAP WATER ONTO IT GENTLY OVER THE BACK OF A SPOON.

SAVING THE SOLUTE

A liquid that dissolves substances is called a solvent. Water dissolves so many different substances, it's the "universal solvent." The substance that dissolves is the solute. Together, solute and solvent form a solution. In the project here you can get back the solute, salt, simply by letting the solvent, water, dry out.

WATER SUPPLY

Imagine you turn on the tap and smelly, slimy, muddy brown water comes out! That would be shocking, harmful, even deadly! Water industries spend billions on filters and other purifying equipment. These supply us with clean, pure water that is safe for washing, cooking, and drinking.

PROJECT: MAKE DIRTY WATER CLEARER

At a treatment plant, water waits first in shallow tanks, so bigger lumps can settle to the bottom.

CLEARING WATER

MAKE SOME MUDDY WATER BY SPOONING GARDEN SOIL INTO A JAR. ADD TAP WATER, PUT ON THE LID, AND SHAKE IT ALL UP.

CAREFULLY CUT SQUARES OF MUSLIN AND OLD TIGHTS MATERIAL. SECURE THESE TO THE TOPS OF TWO JELLY JARS WITH RUBBER BANDS.

PRESS DIMPLES INTO THE MUSLIN AND TIGHTS FILTERS. CURVE THE PAPER TOWEL INTO A CONE FOR THE THIRD FILTER AND FIT IT INTO ITS JAR.

WHAT YOU NEED

- soil
- muslin
- old tights
- paper towel
- sieve
- three jelly jars
- rubber bands
- scissors

HOLEY FILTER!

Each filter material has holes, called mesh. They are largest in the muslin and too small to see in the paper towel. Water can pass easily through the holes, but solid particles cannot. The smaller the holes, the less mud gets through, so the filtered water is clearer.

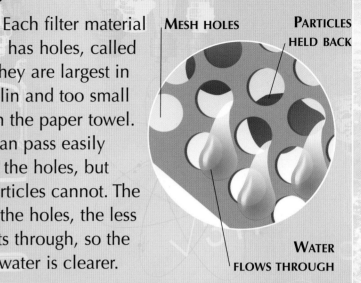

MESH HOLES

PARTICLES HELD BACK

WATER FLOWS THROUGH

MUSLIN
(COARSE MESH)

TIGHTS
(MEDIUM MESH)

PAPER TOWEL
(FINE MESH)

BECOMING CLEARER
FIRST POUR THE MUDDY WATER THROUGH THE SIEVE TO REMOVE SMALL STONES AND LEAVES. THEN POUR EQUAL AMOUNTS THROUGH THE THREE FILTERS. SEE HOW THE WATER IS CLEARER EACH TIME. THIS IS DUE TO THE SIZE OF THE HOLES IN THE FILTERS, AS SHOWN ABOVE.

LOTS OF FILTERS

In a real water-purifying system there are several sets of filters, each with a smaller mesh than the one before. This is because if a very small mesh is used first, it quickly clogs with large particles. (In the project here, you used the sieve as a "pre-filter" to take out the largest bits.)

TRY POURING THE SAME MUDDY WATER FIRST THROUGH THE MUSLIN, THEN THE TIGHTS, THEN THE PAPER TOWEL. COMPARE THE SOLIDS LEFT BEHIND ON THE FILTERS.

CURVED WATER

The curved surface of water, as on this over-full glass, is known as the meniscus.

Sometimes you can put water into a glass o mug, and its level is higher than the rim! The water seems to have a curved "skin" o it. This is due to a characteristic of water called surface tension. It's so strong it can hold up small, light objects.

Small creatures, like this raft spider, can walk across water. This is because they do not break the surface skin of the water.

PROJECT: MAKE SOME WATER WALKERS

FOLD A STRIP OF ALUMINUM FOIL 3/4-INCH BY 14 INCHES INTO A RECTANGLE AROUND A PAPER CLIP.

CAREFULLY CUT TWO DEEP V-SHAPED NOTCHES IN EITHER SIDE, ALMOST AS FAR AS THE PAPER CLIP.

WHAT YOU NEED

- foil
- paper clips
- large, shallow bowl of water
- dish washing liquid
- scissors

FOLD DOWN THE SIX "LEGS." BEND THE ENDS TO MAKE "FEET" THAT REST FLAT ON THE SURFACE.

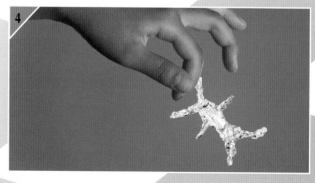

CAREFULLY LOWER THE WATER WALKER INTO SOME WATER WITHOUT BREAKING THE SURFACE.

SKIMMING THE SURFACE
SEE HOW THE FEET OF THE WATER
WALKER MAKE SMALL DIMPLES IN THE
SURFACE. MAKE SEVERAL WALKERS AND
PUSH THEM GENTLY SIDEWAYS. WHEN
ONE COMES NEAR ANOTHER, DOES THE
SECOND ONE MOVE TOO?

STICKY "SKIN"

Water's tiny particles, or molecules, pull or attract each other strongly. Molecules at the surface are pulled from the sides and below, but not above in the air. These unbalanced forces, or tensions, cause a "skin" at the surface.

PULL OR ATTRACTION
BETWEEN WATER
MOLECULES

UNBALANCED
ATTRACTIONS AT THE
SURFACE FORM A "ROOF"

INVISIBLE PUSH

Gather your water walkers together in the bowl's center. Place a drop of washing liquid in the middle. Do they move, and if so, together or apart? The soapy liquid disturbs and "stretches" the water's surface tension.

CREEPING WATER

Water can climb as high as the tallest trees. In fact, it climbs up inside them! Water in a thin pipe acts like "string." As it

Water rises up tiny cracks in wood, brick, or plaster, to cause damp walls.

comes out one end, it pulls more water through from the other end. This feature works only in very narrow tubes, called capillaries. The "creeping" of water along them is known as capillary action.

A tree's roots suck in water from the ground. The water then rises dozens of feet up the micro-thin "living pipes," called xylem tubes, inside the wood of the trunk to the leaves high above.

PROJECT: COLOR A FLOWER

COLOR A FLOWER

WHAT YOU NEED

- flower
- container
- food coloring
- scissors

SNIP OFF THE LOWER STEM OF A WHITE FLOWER LIKE A CARNATION, LEAVING ABOUT 8 INCHES.

FILL A GLASS OR VASE WITH WATER DYED DARK WITH PLENTY OF FOOD COLORING.

PLACE THE CUT FLOWER IN THE COLORED WATER AND LEAVE IT OVERNIGHT.

SUCKER!

Capillary action works only in extremely thin tubes. The water's surface tension (see previous page) makes its edges "creep" along the tube, whether this faces sideways, down, or straight up. The attraction between the water molecules is so strong that they pull more molecules behind them so the whole column of water slides along.

SURFACE CREEPS UP THE TUBE

MENISCUS (CURVE OF SURFACE)

ATTRACTION BETWEEN WATER MOLECULES

TINGED WITH COLOR
THE FLOWER STARTS TO CHANGE COLOR! THE COLORED WATER PASSES UP TINY TUBES IN THE STEM INTO THE PETALS. THE WATER IS GIVEN OFF AS VAPOR LEAVING THE COLOR BEHIND.

RAINBOW BOUQUET

With several white flowers and a selection of different food colorings, you can color each bloom differently, and make a "rainbow bouquet." What happens if you put the flowers back into clear water?

CAREFULLY SLICE A WHITE FLOWER'S STEM LENGTHWAYS ABOUT HALFWAY UP. MAKE TWO GLASSES OF DIFFERENT FOOD COLORS, SIDE BY SIDE. PUT ONE HALF OF THE STEM IN EACH. WHAT HAPPENS TO THE FLOWER?

FLOAT AND SINK

A boat is made of metal but is also full of air. So for its overall volume, it is very light and it can carry huge heavy containers.

Imagine a huge rock that weighed 10,000 tonnes floating on water – never! Yet a ship that heavy floats easily. This is due to displacement. When an object is put into water it pushes away, or displaces, some of the water. If this amount of water weighs less than the object, the object sinks. If the displaced water weighs more, the object floats. This is called buoyancy.

As water leaks into a boat, it replaces air. The boat becomes heavier and finally sinks.

PROJECT: MAKE A BOAT FLOAT

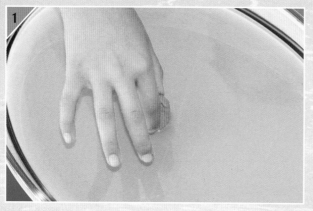

ROLL A LUMP OF MODELING CLAY INTO A BALL. PUT IT INTO THE WATER. DOES IT FLOAT?

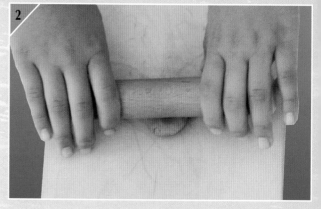

ROLL THE BALL INTO A THIN, FLAT SHEET WITH A SIMPLE BOAT SHAPE, POINTED AT ONE END.

GIVING A PUSH UP

An object put into water pushes aside, or displaces, some of the water. This displaced water pushes back on the object with an opposing force which is equal to its own weight. If a solid object weighing 2 pounds is altered into a hollow shape, it now has a larger volume for the same weight (most of its volume is now air). So it displaces more water, making the opposing force greater—and it floats.

SOLID OBJECT WEIGHS 2 POUNDS

WATER DISPLACED WEIGHS 1 POUND

LESS OPPOSING FORCE, SOLID OBJECT SINKS

HOLLOW OBJECT WEIGHS 2 POUNDS

WATER DISPLACED WEIGHS 3 POUNDS

MORE OPPOSING FORCE, HOLLOW OBJECT FLOATS

FROM SINKER TO FLOATER
THE CLAY WEIGHS THE SAME, BUT NOW IT'S A HOLLOW BOAT SHAPE, IT FLOATS (SEE ABOVE).

HEAVY LOAD

Make a short groove in the side of the boat, exactly level with the water's surface as it floats. Now add some "cargo" to the boat, like wooden blocks. These make the boat heavier. Does it float lower in the water?

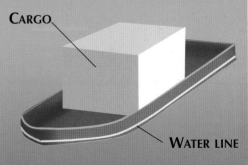

CARGO

WATER LINE

TRY PUTTING THE BOAT ON VERY SALTY WATER (PAGE 12). DOES IT FLOAT LOWER OR HIGHER?

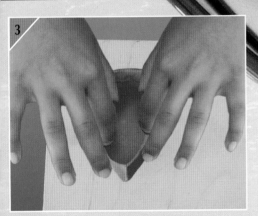

3

PINCH UP THE EDGES ALL AROUND TO MAKE WATERTIGHT SIDES FOR THE BOAT.

4

GENTLY PLACE THE BOAT ON THE WATER'S SURFACE. WHAT HAPPENS?

UNDER PRESSURE

If a party balloon was taken to the bottom of the sea, it would be compressed smaller than a pea! Water is heavy, and the deeper you go, the more water there is above to press on you. This water pressure can compress gases like air into a tiny space and so change their buoyancy.

Like the model diver here, a real scuba diver tends to rise slightly when breathing in and sink a little when breathing out.

Submarines have especially strong bodies, or hulls, that resist the incredible water pressure under the sea.

PROJECT: MAKE A DEEP DIVER

DEEP DIVER

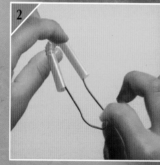

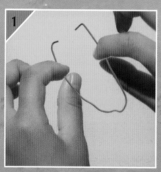

STRAIGHTEN A LARGE PAPER CLIP. CURL IT INTO A LONG U-SHAPE. BEND THE ENDS IN SLIGHTLY.

TRIM A FLEXIBLE STRAW TO LEAVE THE FLEXIBLE PART. INSERT THE ENDS OF THE PAPER CLIP U INTO IT.

WHAT YOU NEED

- large paper clip
- flexible straw
- drink bottle
- jelly jar
- water
- modeling clay
- scissors

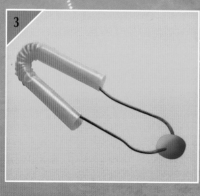

ATTACH A SMALL LUMP OF MODELING CLAY TO THE BOTTOM OF THE PAPER CLIP U.

PUT THE DIVER IN THE JAR OF WATER. ALTER THE AMOUNT OF CLAY SO THE DIVER JUST FLOATS.

NOW PUT THE DIVER INTO THE BOTTLE OF WATER. SCREW ON THE TOP TIGHTLY.

SQUEEZED SMALLER

The diver just floats because the amount of water it displaces weighs the same as it does (see previous page). Squeezing the bottle increases the pressure on the water. Water itself cannot be compressed. But the air trapped as small pockets in the straw is squeezed smaller. As this happens, extra water enters the straw and makes the whole diver heavier, so it sinks. Relieving the pressure allows the air to expand and push the water out, so the diver becomes lighter.

AIR BUBBLES INSIDE BENDY PART OF STRAW

PAPER CLIP

PRESSURE OF THE WATER

PRESSURE OF THE WATER

MODELING CLAY ADJUSTS BUOYANCY

DIVE! DIVE! DIVE!
SQUEEZE THE SIDES OF THE BOTTLE—AND THE DIVER DESCENDS! GENTLY TAKE THE PRESSURE OFF BY LETTING GO OF THE SIDES AND IT SHOULD RISE AGAIN. TRY THIS SEVERAL TIMES. WHAT HAPPENS IF YOU TIP THE WHOLE BOTTLE UPSIDE DOWN?

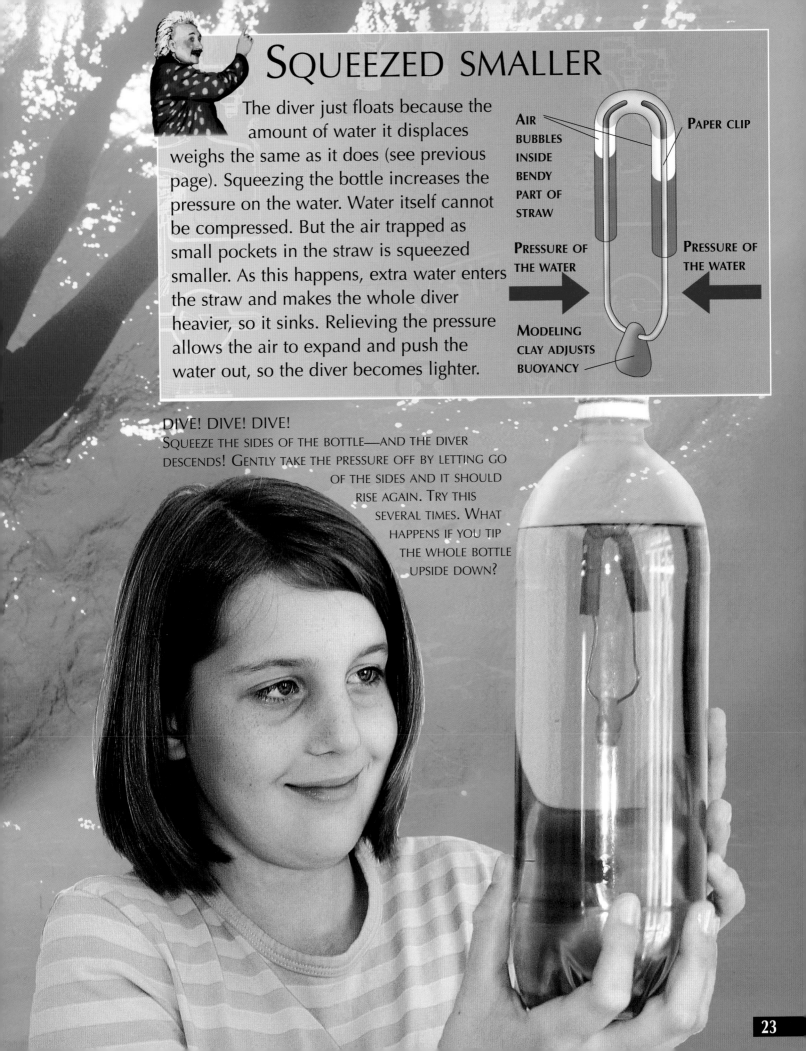

WATER FORCE

Squeeze air and it gets smaller. Squeeze water and it doesn't. If you press water at one end of a pipe, the water itself presses back all along the pipe and at the other end. This is the science of hydraulics, and it's very useful.

Early hydraulic machines used water as their liquid. But modern versions like this backhoe use thick, slippery hydraulic oil instead.

Liquid force can be used for absorbing shocks like the hydraulic oil used in car shock absorbers.

PROJECT: MAKE WATER LIFT A LOAD

WATER LIFTER

WHAT YOU NEED

- **two drink bottles**
- **balloon**
- **straw**
- **jar lid**
- **modeling clay**
- **water**
- **glue**
- **scissors**

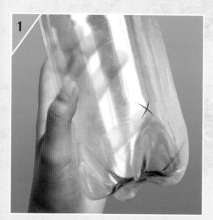

1 CAREFULLY TRIM THE TOPS OFF TWO IDENTICAL DRINK BOTTLES. MAKE A SMALL STAR-SHAPED CUT IN THE LOWER SIDE OF EACH.

2 CUT A LENGTH OF STRAW AND INSERT EACH END INTO ONE OF THE STAR CUTS TO JOIN THE BOTTLES TOGETHER.

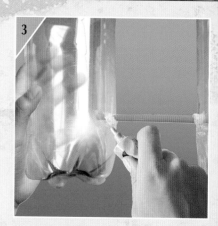

3 PUT PLENTY OF PLASTIC-ADHESIVE GLUE AROUND EACH STRAW END TO SEAL IT FIRMLY TO THE BOTTLE. LEAVE OVERNIGHT.

PUSHING POWER

The balloon in the bottle works like a hydraulic piston in a cylinder. The water's pressure is carried, or transmitted, all through it to every part of its surface. This changes a "down" force in one bottle into an "up" force in the other.

PISTON PRESSES DOWN **WATER IS PUSHED THROUGH THE STRAW** **LOAD LIFTED UP**

UPWARD FORCE

BIG AND SMALL

Pressure is force over a certain area. More area = more force. Try two different bottles, large and small. Press in the small one—is there extra force in the large one?

HALF-FILL THE BOTTLES WITH WATER, FLOWING INTO THE STRAW. PUT AN UPTURNED JAR LID IN ONE BOTTLE.

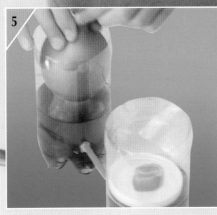

ADD MODELING CLAY TO THE JAR LID. NOW PLACE A BALLOON INSIDE THE OTHER BOTTLE AND INFLATE SO THAT IT PRESSES AGAINST THE SIDES.

HOMEMADE HYDRAULICS
AS YOU PUSH THE BALLOON DOWN, IT PRESSES ON THE WATER SURFACE BELOW. THIS FORCES THE WATER DOWN IN ONE BOTTLE, ALONG THE STRAW AND UP INTO THE OTHER BOTTLE—EASILY LIFTING THE LID AND CLAY.

WATER POWER

Anything that moves has energy, the type called kinetic energy. We harness flowing water's kinetic energy directly using a waterwheel, for movement tasks such as lifting heavy loads or turning millstones to grind grain. Scientists also know that energy can be changed from one form to another. This happens at a hydroelectric power station, where water's kinetic energy is converted into electricity.

Before engines and motors, waterwheels drove all kinds of machines.

PROJECT: BUILD A WATERWHEEL

WATERWHEEL

WHAT YOU NEED

- **cardboard mailing tube**
- **flexible straws**
- **modeling clay**
- **cardboard**
- **acrylic paint**
- **foam board**
- **string**
- **funnel**
- **glue**
- **scissors**
- **craft knife**

1 CUT A SHORT "DRUM" OF STRONG CARDBOARD TUBE (LIKE A MAILING TUBE). PUT THE END CAPS BACK ON.

2 CAREFULLY CUT A SMALL HOLE IN THE CENTER OF EACH END CAP, JUST BIG ENOUGH FOR THE STRAW TO FIT IN.

3 TRIM A LENGTH OF STRAW FOR THE AXLE. ROLL A THIN "ROD" OF MODELING CLAY TO FIT INSIDE THE STRAW.

4 THREAD THE CLAY ROD INTO THE STRAW. PUSH MORE CLAY INTO EACH END SO THE CLAY FILLS THE WHOLE STRAW.

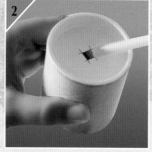

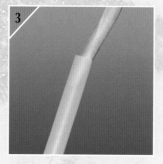

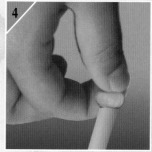

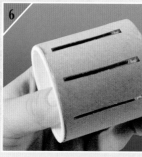

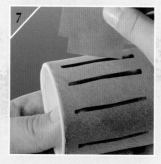

5 PUSH THE STRAW THROUGH THE HOLES AND GLUE. LEAVE MORE STRAW ON ONE SIDE THAN THE OTHER.

6 CUT EIGHT EQUALLY SPACED SLOTS INTO THE DRUM RIM, EACH WIDE ENOUGH TO HOLD THE THICK CARDBOARD.

7 FROM THE CARDBOARD, CUT EIGHT RECTANGLES WITH TABS AS PADDLES. PUSH THEM FIRMLY INTO THE DRUM RIM'S SLOTS.

8 TRIM TWO TRIANGLES AND ONE SQUARE OF FOAM BOARD, TO MAKE THE BASE. GLUE IT TOGETHER.

IN A SPIN

The force of gravity gives the water kinetic energy. As the water hits the waterwheel, it transfers its energy to the paddles. This produces rotary motion by making the waterwheel spin on its axle.

FALLING WATER

SPINNING MOTION

WHAT A WIND-UP! POUR WATER INTO THE FUNNEL. IT FALLS ONTO THE PADDLES, SPINS THE WATERWHEEL, AND WINDS UP THE WEIGHT. EXPERIMENT BY TILTING THE FUNNEL FOR THE MOST WINDING POWER.

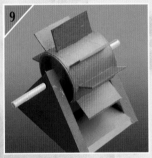

9

10

PAINT THE WHEEL WITH ACRYLIC PAINT. CUT HOLES IN THE TRIANGLES FOR THE AXLE AND FIX THE WHEEL TO THE BASE.

REMOVE ONE SIDE FROM A BOX. CUT A HOLE IN THE TOP FOR A FUNNEL. GLUE THE WATERWHEEL BASE TO THE BOTTOM.

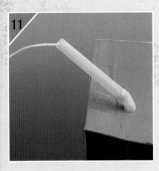

11

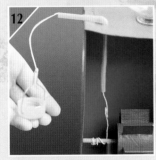

12

CUT A SMALL HOLE IN THE BOX TOP FOR A BENDY STRAW. THREAD STRING THROUGH THE STRAW AS SHOWN.

TIE ONE STRING END TO THE LONGER SIDE OF THE AXLE, THE OTHER TO A SMALL WEIGHT OUTSIDE THE BOX.

PADDLE SHAPES

Make another waterwheel with differently shaped paddles, such as the cardboard shape bent at an angle. You could even glue several small plastic cups around the drum. See which design lifts the heaviest weight.

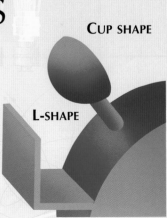

CUP SHAPE

L-SHAPE

WATER PROPULSION

Because water is a liquid, it flows when pushed. However, pushing water is difficult because it pushes back with a force called resistance. To move through water fast, you need powerful propulsion. Boats use oars, sails, paddles, or a propeller-like screw.

A huge boat like a cruise ship or an oil tanker has a huge screw over 60 feet across.

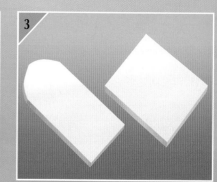

A catamaran or "cat" has two long, narrow, sharp-nosed hulls which reduce water resistance.

PROJECT: MAKE A POWERBOAT

POWERBOAT

WHAT YOU NEED

- **setting clay**
- **thick foam board**
- **stiff wire**
- **plastic beads**
- **rubber band**
- **craft knife**
- **pliers**
- **acrylic paint**

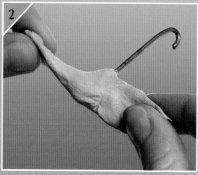

1 BEND ONE END OF A SHORT, STRAIGHT PIECE OF WIRE INTO A HOOK SHAPE AND THE OTHER END INTO AN L-SHAPE.

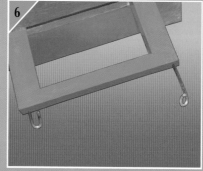

2 MAKE A PROPELLER OR SCREW (SEE OPPOSITE) AROUND THE L-SHAPED END, USING HARDENING OR SETTING CLAY. LEAVE TO SET.

3 FROM THICK FOAM BOARD, CUT A BOAT-LIKE HULL SHAPE AND A RECTANGULAR PIECE FOR THE KEEL BELOW.

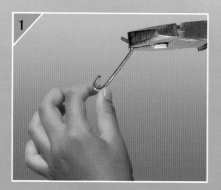

5 TAKE TWO LENGTHS OF WIRE. BEND THE END OF ONE INTO A HOOK. PAINT THE BOAT.

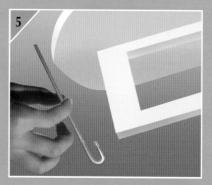

6 BEND THE OTHER WIRE'S END INTO A LOOP. PUSH THEM INTO THE KEEL, LOOP AT THE REAR.

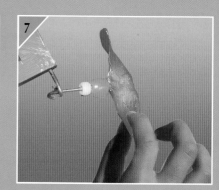

7 THREAD TWO BEADS ONTO THE PROPELLER SHAFT AND INSERT IT THROUGH THE WIRE LOOP.

TWIST INTO PUSH

As the screw's angled blades spin, they push the water and the water's resistance pushes back to propel the boat forward. Also, if the front surface of each blade is curved and the rear surface is flat, water passes faster over the front surface. This creates lower pressure in front and "sucks" the screw forward.

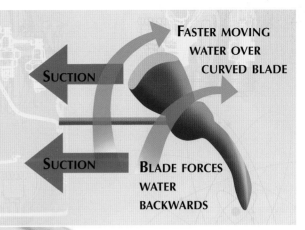

FASTER MOVING WATER OVER CURVED BLADE

SUCTION

SUCTION

BLADE FORCES WATER BACKWARDS

SCREW SHAPE
EACH BLADE OF THE SCREW IS ANGLED ON THE HUB. IT WIDENS GRADUALLY FROM THE HUB, WITH A ROUNDED END.

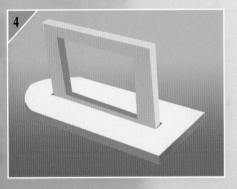

4

CUT A LARGE "WINDOW" IN THE KEEL. CUT A SLOT INTO THE HULL JUST BIG ENOUGH FOR THE KEEL EDGE, AND PUSH THIS INTO PLACE.

GOING FOR A SPIN
LAUNCH THE BOAT. IT GOES FORWARD OR BACKWARD, DEPENDING ON WHICH WAY YOU WOUND UP THE SCREW!

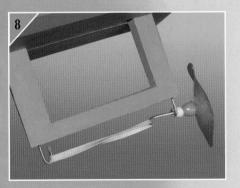

8

STRETCH A RUBBER BAND BETWEEN THE TWO HOOKS. TURN THE SCREW TO WIND UP THE RUBBER BAND.

SCREW OR PADDLES?

Try adapting the waterwheel shown on the previous page, and adding a rubber band, to make a paddleboat. Notice how the paddles turn partly in air and how water splashes around. All this is wasted energy.

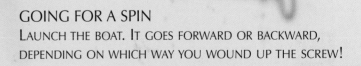

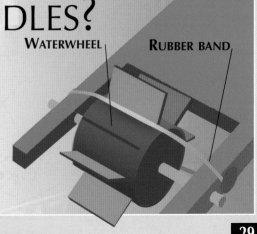

WATERWHEEL

RUBBER BAND

HISTORY OF WATER

335 B.C.E. In ancient Greece, the famous scientist and thinker Aristotle described the belief that water was one of the four "elements" from which all other substances were made. The other three were air, fire, and earth. These views lasted for about 2,000 years.

1724 Gabriel Fahrenheit described how water could be "supercooled" or chilled below its freezing point for a short time without turning into ice. He also devised the Fahrenheit scale of temperature, where water freezes at 32 °F and boils at 212 °F.

1742 Anders Celsius devised a scale of temperature using water's freezing point as 100 and its boiling point as 0. A few years later his colleagues changed it round to 0 and 100, and it became the Celsius scale, °C.

1783 Gaspard Monge, a math expert, made water by combining oxygen and hydrogen gases. He later worked with Lavoisier on "making and breaking" water.

1784 Henry Cavendish exploded a mixture of hydrogen gas and air and produced a substance that "seemed pure water." Making water in this way caused scientists to doubt it was a pure element.

1785 Lavoisier did more work on Cavendish's experiments to show that water is a combination of hydrogen and oxygen.

1800 Anthony Carlisle and William Nicholson used electricity to split water into hydrogen and oxygen gases by the process of electrolysis.

1805 Joseph Gay-Lussac proved that water is made of two parts hydrogen and one part oxygen. The chemical formula of water is H_2O.

1933 Gilbert Lewis made "heavy water" D_2O, where hydrogen is replaced by a similar chemical, deuterium. This substance is very important in atomic chain reactions and nuclear power stations.

1996 NASA space scientists announced that water was present on the moon, frozen in the rocks.

2003 The Mars Exploration Rover Mission landed two space probes on the surface of Mars to look for evidence of liquid water that may have once been on the surface of the planet. Frozen water is found at the martian poles. Photographic evidence suggests that Mars may have had water just like we have on earth today.

GLOSSARY

Boil when a liquid substance is heated so much that it changes into a gas. Most substances do this if hot enough, even metals like iron

Condense when a substance cools and changes from a gas or vapor into liquid form

Density amount of matter of a substance, usually measured as mass or weight, in a certain volume

Dissolve when a substance, the solute, "breaks apart" into its tiniest pieces and floats around in a solvent such as water, forming a solution

Evaporate when a substance changes from a liquid to a gas

Expand to become larger and take up more volume, for example, when a substance is heated

Freezing when a substance changes from liquid form into a solid. Most substances freeze if they are cold enough, even gases like oxygen and nitrogen from the air.

Liquid substance that can change shape easily and move or flow, but which usually cannot be compressed (squeezed smaller)

Molecules two or more atoms joined together to make the smallest pieces or particles of most everyday substances and materials

Solute substance that dissolves in a solvent to form a solution

Solution substance containing a solute that has dissolved into a solvent

Solvent substance in which a solute dissolves to form a solution

Water cycle cyclical movement of water in its various forms, from seas and oceans, up to clouds, down as rain and snow, and across the ground in streams and rivers

Water vapor invisible, gas form of water

INDEX